QUEENSLAND
NATIONAL PARKS

Photography by Geoff Higgins

Text by Dalys Newman

WOOLLAHRA

PRECEDING PAGE: The wreck of the *Cherry Venture*, a small coastal steamer flung ashore in a storm in 1973, can be seen at Cooloola National Park. The park covers 56 000 hectares, conserving a large tract of natural land on Queensland's southern coast.

ABOVE: Rolling expanses of sand dunes on Fraser Island, part of the Great Sandy National Park.

BELOW LEFT: Washed ashore during a cyclone in 1935, the *Maheno* is an impressive wreck north of Happy Valley on Fraser Island.

BELOW RIGHT AND OPPOSITE: Rainforest pockets dotted throughout Fraser Island in Queensland are dense with huge kauri, rough-barked satinay, brush box and hundreds of airy piccabeen palms. The island was heavily logged during the 20th century but the timber industry ceased in 1992 when it attained World Heritage listing. Fraser's rainforests are also home to rare and ancient species including the angiopteris fern.

OPPOSITE: Curtis Falls in Joalah National Park on the Tamborine plateau where rain-fed mountain streams have carved deep gorges and spectacular waterfalls into the region's volcanic rocks.

ABOVE: Lake McKenzie on Fraser Island is an example of a perched fresh-water lake. These lakes are formed when a saucer-shaped hard pad of organic debris, sand and peat forms in a depression between sand dunes. Water cannot penetrate the pad and collects, well above the water table.

CENTRE: Transport is by 4WD on Fraser Island, which is less than an hour's ride by boat or barge from the mainland.

RIGHT: The Pinnacles, sculpted sand dunes on Fraser Island. The dune systems of the Great Sandy Region, which include Fraser Island, are the largest and the oldest in the world, dating back more than 30 000 years. Stretching 123 kilometres along Queensland's southern coast, Fraser is the world's largest sand island. More than 98 per cent of its 165 280 hectares is part of the larger Great Sandy National Park.

ABOVE: Carlo Sandblow in the Cooloola National Park is a popular launching pad for hang-gliding enthusiasts. Sandblows are caused through the gradual action of shifting sand.

ABOVE RIGHT: Sand dunes run down to the sea in Cooloola National Park. A chain of sand islands and long sand beaches on the mainland, all backed by dunes, begins at South Stradbroke Island and extends to Sandy Cape at the northern tip of Fraser Island.

RIGHT: The Girraween National Park, situated at the northern end of the New England Tableland, protects the catchment area of the Bald Rock Creek with its clear streams and granite cascades.

OPPOSITE AND OVERLEAF: Girraween National Park, with an average elevation of 900 metres, is a place of massive granite outcrops, large angular tors and precariously balanced rocks. Millions of years ago, erupting volcanoes formed a granite mass which has been weathered over the years to create boulder-strewn hills and valleys. Nowhere else in eastern Australia is there massive granite hills and boulder clusters in such abundance.

ABOVE: Grass trees at Bunya National Park. These extremely slow-growing plants have a lifespan of 600 years. They grow to a height of 4 metres with a growth rate of about 1 metre every hundred years.

ABOVE RIGHT: Sunlight spotlights a fern in the Bunya Mountain National Park. Dry subtropical rainforest, once the most widespread rainforest community in Queensland, grows on the eastern side of the mountains in this spectacular park.

CENTRE RIGHT: The Bunya Mountains support the largest remaining area of bunya pines, recognizable by their distinctive dome-shaped crowns. Rising dramatically from the surrounding plains, the Bunya's peaks average 975 metres above sea level. Geologists believe the mountains to be 30 million years old, the remains of an old volcano.

RIGHT: Elebana Falls in Lamington National Park. Fertile volcanic soils and the variability of rainfall in this 20 200 hectare park yield a lush environment of diverse vegetation including mist-shrouded cool temperate rainforest and the largest preserved stand of sub-tropical rainforest in Australia.

LEFT: Natural Bridge (also called Natural Arch) is one of the highlights of the 2954 hectare Springbrook National Park, near the Queensland–New South Wales border. The rock archway spans the mountain-fed waters of Cave Creek and is surrounded by lush sub-tropical rainforest. The creek once flowed over a waterfall, the base of which had softer rock than the surrounding area. Over time, churning water eroded this softer rock and gouged out a cavern. A pothole gradually developed in the creek above and deepened until it broke through the cavern roof. The remaining rock resembles a natural bridge.

BELOW: Spectacular Carnarvon Gorge in the 298 000 hectare Carnarvon Gorge National Park is a lush oasis in the rugged ranges of Queensland's central highlands. The 200 metre high and 400 metre wide gorge formed millions of years ago when, over countless seasons, the waters of Carnarvon Creek carved through the sandstone foothills of the Great Dividing Range.

OPPOSITE: The moss garden in Carnarvon Gorge is carpeted with green moss and a waterfall scatters the surrounding rocks with a myriad of tiny droplets. Within the gorge, Carnarvon Creek flows year-round, giving life to luxuriant vegetation which supports diverse native animals, including birds, kangaroos and platypus.

BELOW: The Chimneys in the Mt Moffatt section of Carnarvon Gorge National Park are stunning examples of erosion of sandstone beneath a basalt cap.

RIGHT: Sites such as Baloon Cave, Cathedral Cave and the Art Gallery in Carnarvon Gorge National Park offer some of the country's finest examples of Aboriginal stencil art. Lower walls are covered by hundreds of stencils and paintings of human features and implements.

BELOW RIGHT: The Carnarvon National Park is a bushwalkers' paradise. The sandstone gorge snakes 30 kilometres through an otherwise dry landscape.

BOTTOM RIGHT: The dramatic shapes of old volcanic plugs stand sentinel in the Peak Range National Park. The plugs were formed when the volcanoes cooled and the molten lava melted in the volcanic pipe.

OPPOSITE AND ABOVE: Two Mile Falls flows through Blackdown Tableland National Park, which rises above the hot, dry plains of central Queensland. The park comprises a sandstone plateau with sheer cliffs, deep gorges, tall eucalypt forest, heath, spectacular waterfalls, wild-flowers and Aboriginal rock art. In sheltered areas, ferns and mosses thrive in the moist environments created by the plateau's streams.

BELOW: Blackdown Tableland was given its name in 1869 by William Yaldwin who named it after Blackdown House, his family home in Sussex. In 1982, 23 000 hectares of the tableland was gazetted as national park for its outstanding conservation and scenic values. There are many excellent views from lookouts at the edge of the escarpment, such as Horseshoe Lookout (pictured), Rainbow Falls and Stony Creek Falls. The plateau is about 600 metres above the surrounding area and is bordered by precipitous cliffs rising to 350 metres.

ABOVE AND CENTRE: Lawn Hill Creek, in Lawn Hill National Park, winds through the ancient ramparts of the Constance Range on its way to the Gulf of Carpentaria. Bordered by sheer red, orange and grey cliffs and surrounded by lush tropical vegetation, the creek is a remote oasis in the dry plains of northern Queensland.

BELOW: Lush, tropical vegetation around Lawn Hill Creek includes cabbage palms, Leichardt pines, paperbarks, figs and white cedar trees. Eucalypts and spinifex grasslands dot the surrounding plateau.

OPPOSITE: Lawn Hill Gorge winds for 3 kilometres through the Lawn Hill National Park, its massive walls rising 60 metres above the creek. The gorge ends at the Island Stack, an imposing rock plug formed by the creek as it changes course. The park covers 12 200 hectares of mostly sparsely vegetated, terraced plateau on the edge of the Barkly Tableland.

LEFT: Some of Australia's most easterly wind-blown sand dunes are to be found in Welford National Park. These sweeping red dunes in the western part of the park contrast dramatically with the stark ghost gums and the flush of greenery and wild-flowers after rain.

BELOW: The Barcoo River forms the southern boundary of the 124 000 hectare Welford National Park. Made a national park in 1992, Welford conserves a diverse range of plants and landscapes of the Mulga region. Stately river red gums, ghost gums, spinifex plains and gidgee scrub are all found in the park and the rugged northern and eastern sections are home to the rare yellow-footed wallaby which finds shelter in the rocky outcrops and large boulders of the area.

TOP LEFT: Towering cliffs of spectacularly coloured sandstone are reflected in cool creek waters in Porcupine Gorge National Park. Here, wind and water have coloured and eroded the sandstone, forming fluted channels, boulders, potholes and shallow caves. The canyon walls reveal strata of sedimentary rock spanning hundreds of millions of years of geological history.

CENTRE LEFT: Dunes, coastal scrub and rainforest are features of the 800 hectare Cape Hillsborough National Park, north-east of Mackay. The park conserves eucalypt forest, hoop pine, creeks, mangroves, hills and headlands and supports over 150 species of birdlife and tropical butterflies. Kangaroos, wallabies and bush turkeys can often be seen on the beaches.

LEFT: Wedge Island can be reached from the beach at Cape Hillsborough National Park at low tide.

ABOVE: Pyramid Rock, a striking monolith of multi-coloured sandstone, rises from the floor of the gorge in Porcupine Gorge National Park.

LEFT: Missionary Bay at Hinchinbrook Island National Park. Steep gorge-like valleys slope outwards from the high, rainforest-covered ridges of this mountain range that looms out of the sea. With an area of more than 39 000 hectares, Hinchinbrook is Australia's largest island national park.

LEFT: Alligator Creek flows through Bowling Green Bay National Park. This large, diverse 55 300 hectare park contains the rugged Mt Elliot area, tropical rainforest, woodland and coastal wetlands, saltpans and mangroves.

BELOW LEFT: The Paradise Waterhole at Paluma Range National Park, north-west of Townsville. This mountainous park features dense tropical rainforest, open forest and panoramic views. It is a wet tropics World Heritage area containing some of the oldest continuously surviving rainforest on earth and many rare and endangered plants and animals.

BOTTOM LEFT: Waterfalls cascade over salmon-coloured rocks and huge water-smoothed boulders in Jourama Falls National Park. Palms, umbrella trees and figs fringe the creek, freshwater tortoises sun themselves on rocks and goannas can often be seen scuttling into the vegetation.

OPPOSITE: Crystal Cascades in Eungella National Park, high in central Queensland's Clarke Range. The 52 000 hectare park protects unique animals and an unusual combination of tropical and subtropical vegetation. More than a thousand plant species, many rare or threatened, have been recorded here and the park is home to several animal species recorded nowhere else in the country. Situated at the top of the Pioneer Valley, west of Mackay, Eungella takes its name from the local Aboriginal word for 'cloud'.

OPPOSITE AND TOP RIGHT: Rainforest species flourish in the tropical climate of Eungella National Park. Eungella's rainforests have been isolated by dry corridors of open eucalypt forest for over 30 000 years, creating a fascinating evolutionary experiment.

RIGHT: The Great Barrier Reef Marine Park, covering about 345 000 square kilometres, is the world's largest marine protected area. Stretching about 2000 kilometres along the north-east coast of Queensland, the Great Barrier Reef is the world's largest and most complex reef system and one of the most biologically diverse systems on earth. With its myriad of individual coral reefs and continental islands, reef islands and cays, it provides a habitat for many rare and endangered species and has been described as the 'eighth' natural wonder of the world.

RIGHT: The clear waters of Davies Creek flow over the rugged granite outcrops in Davies Creek National Park, west of Cairns. This small 480 hectare park contains huge granite boulders eroded over millions of years to create spectacular formations, the Davies Creek Falls and water slides.

BELOW RIGHT: Gaunt, pinnacled limestone towers project up to 70 metres above the surrounding plains in the 1876 hectare Chillagoe–Mungana Caves National Park, west of Cairns. These huge, dark grey edifices are part of an eroded limestone belt, undercut by many kilometres of caves decorated with interesting flowstone formations. The limestone was deposited approximately 400 million years ago on the bed of a shallow sea. Since then, major earth movements have folded and tilted it into an almost vertical position.

OVERLEAF: Complex mesophyll vine forest with lawyer vine in the canopy and scattered granite boulders are features of Babinda Creek Boulders Wildland Park.

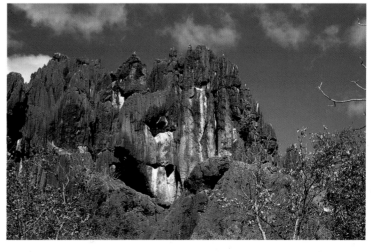

ABOVE: The Beatrice River flows through dense rainforest in the Palmerston National Park, south of Cairns. Here, several walking trails lead to lookouts and waterfalls and tracks zig-zag down into gorges along the river.

BELOW LEFT: Richly coloured stalactites, stalagmites, shawls, canopies, crystal flows, rimstone pools and pendants are found in the labyrinthine caves and tunnels in Chillagoe–Mungana Caves National Park. Numerous species of bats roost and breed in the caves, and the grey swiftlet, a bird with an echo-location system, also nests here.

BELOW RIGHT: The boulders, in Babinda Creek Boulders Wildland Park, are a series of large rocks worn smooth by tropical rains. Since 1959 over 15 people have drowned in the strong currents of this stretch of water. The area also has important significance in Aboriginal legend.

OPPOSITE: Dinner Falls cascade over rocks in an attractive forest setting in the 364 hectare Mt Hypipamee National Park on the Atherton Tableland in northern Queensland. Trees here include black pine and kauri pine.

OPPOSITE: Millstream Falls, the widest falls in Australia, spill over an old basalt lava flow. Though only 20 metres high, the falls reach a width of 60 metres and carry an impressive flow of water right through the dry season. The dry open woodland vegetation here, in the rain shadow of the eastern dividing ranges, offers a stark contrast to the dense rainforest only a few kilometres away.

ABOVE: Little Millstream Falls in the Millstream Falls National Park in northern Queensland. A track leads to the swimming hole at the base of the falls and platypuses are often seen in this area.

CENTRE RIGHT: Palmerston National Park conserves high, dense rainforest, deep gorges, rivers, waterfalls and abundant birdlife. Treelets and shrubs below 5 metres in height make up the shrub layer of this tropical rainforest and the ground layer nurtures herbs, ferns, seedlings and fungi.

BOTTOM RIGHT: Henrietta Creek, a popular picnic and swimming spot in Palmerston National Park.

ABOVE: The ferry service across the Daintree River in the Daintree National Park has been running since the 1950s. This 76 000 hectare park is an important part of the wet tropics of Queensland World Heritage area, declared for its outstanding natural features.

CENTRE LEFT: Rainforest extends right down to the sea near Cape Tribulation. Here, the mountain slopes lift the moist air to build stormy clouds that envelop the highest peaks. With these high ranges so close to the sea, this area experiences some of Australia's highest rainfalls.

BOTTOM LEFT: Four-wheel drive territory —the Daintree National Park. Two of the world's richest ecosystems can be found in this area—lush rainforests and coral reefs. The forests here are home to rare and threatened wildlife, including Bennett's and Lumholtz's tree-kangaroos and southern cassowaries.

RIGHT: Water froths over the smooth granite boulders of the Mossman River in the Daintree National Park. This lower part of Mossman Gorge is one of the few places in the rugged and inaccessible park that can easily be visited.

LEFT: Waterlilies at Lakefield National Park, west of Cooktown. This low-lying area, featuring river channels, billabongs and swamps, is one of Australia's major wetlands. During the wet season, in mid-summer, many rivers flood, spreading their waters across the plains. With the onset of the dry season a mosaic of pools and swamps remain providing a popular habitat for waterbirds.

BELOW: The Cape Tribulation rainforests are of immense biological importance, containing a number of primitive flowering species which are extremely rare. Among the discoveries has been a primitive type of tree, now named *Idiospermium australiense*, which occurs nowhere else in the world. Australia is fortunate in possessing some beautiful remnants of relatively undisturbed rainforest with its diverse range of plants and animals, but in the past 200 years of settlement half of Australia's rainforest has disappeared due to commercial and residential exploitation. In 1981 the Australian Conservation Foundation accorded rainforests major priority status and much has since been achieved in the protection of these unique ecosystems.